40

DAYS 40

BITES

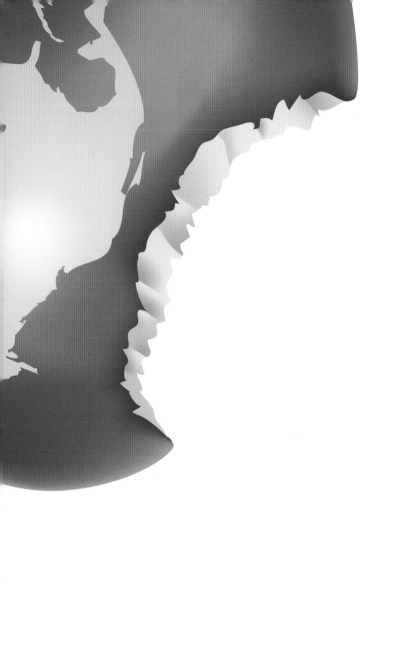

40 DAYS
40 BITES

A FAMILY GUIDE TO PRAY FOR THE WORLD

Trudi Parkes

WORLD CHANGERS

CF4•K

10 9 8 7 6 5 4 3 2 1

© Copyright 2014 Trudi Parkes

ISBN 978-1-78191-401-4

Published in 2014 by Christian Focus Publications, Geanies House, Fearn, Tain, Ross-shire, IV20 1TW , U.K.

Cover design by Daniel van Straaten

Printed and bound in China

Population figures have been rounded to the nearest million.

Scriptures quoted from the International Children's Bible, New Century Version [Anglicised Edition] Copyright © 1991 by Nelson Word Ltd, Milton Keynes, England. Used by permission.

Many of the statistics in this book were taken from *Operation World* Copyright © 2010 by Jason Mandryk. Published by InterVarsity Press, www.ivpress.com.

USE THIS GUIDE TO PRAY FOR THE WORLD EVERY DAY FOR 40 DAYS OR ONCE A WEEK ON A SPECIAL DAY.

THIS BOOK BELONGS TO

AND I AM GOING TO PRAY FOR THE WORLD!

CONTENTS

DAY 1: ALGERIA

Algeria is the largest country in the continent of Africa. It is in North Africa and it borders the Mediterranean Sea. Most Algerians live along the coastal areas of the country as 80% of its land is covered in desert [the Sahara]. Most people in Algeria are Muslims but over the last ten years many have been turning to Jesus. This has been an answer to many years of prayer. Some believe that there could now be over 100,000 Christians.

'We thank God because we have heard about the faith you have in Christ Jesus…You learned about this hope when you heard the true teaching, the Good News that was told to you.'
Colossians 1:4-6

MEET AMINA

An Algerian girl called Amina was ten years old when her friend invited her to a meeting where a Christian woman showed Christian films and had sewing classes for young girls. She heard the gospel for the first time but then her family stopped her going again. During the following years, she struggled with life and family problems. However, when Amina was a young adult she met the Christian woman again. The woman invited Amina to a Christian camp for young people. At the camp Amina was so amazed to hear about God's love and that she could have a personal relationship with him, that she then gave her life to Jesus.

GIVE YOUR LIFE TO JESUS

Flag of Algeria

PRAY:

- For the Algerian church to continue to grow.

- For the many Algerians living in Europe to also hear the gospel.

DID YOU KNOW? The national dish of Algeria is couscous, which is a North African pasta made of wheat!

FACT FILE
Population: 35 million
Main Religion: Islam

Capital: Algiers
Official Languages: Arabic, Berber

ON THE MAP

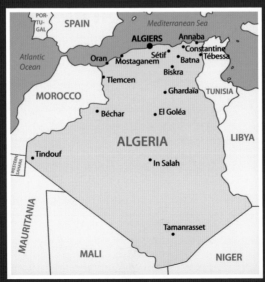

DAY 2: TRANSLATION

When we go to a Christian bookshop we see many different types and versions of the English Bible for sale. It's often difficult to choose which one to buy. It is therefore surprising to find out that there are hundreds of millions of people who can't get Bibles in the language that they understand the best.

'Then I looked, and there was a great number of people. There were so many people that no one could count them. They were from every nation, tribe, people, and language of the earth. They were all standing before the throne and before the Lamb.'
Revelation 7:9

God speaks to us through the Bible but unless people have the Bible in their own language, they cannot read about God's love for them and his message of life and hope.

There are over 200 million people in the world speaking around 2,000 languages who are still waiting for their first verse of the Bible!

MEET JOSIAS

GOD SPEAKS THROUGH THE BIBLE

Josias from Burkina Faso, worked on translating the New Testament into the Bissa Lebir language. After it was printed, churches began to preach, study and sing in the Bissa Lebir language. This caused a revival among the Bissa Lebir people and eight years later the number of churches in the area had risen by 50%.

NEW WORDS: ★ Revival - to bring back to life. ★ Translating - taking words from one language and changing them into another language.

PRAY:

- For God to help people to translate the Bible.

- For more people to do this important work.

DID YOU KNOW? There are over 6,909 languages spoken in the world. Can you say 'hello' in another language? Hola [Spanish] Bonjour [French] Olá [Portuguese].

WORLD CHANGERS 2,000 languages are still waiting for their first verse of the Bible!

DAY 3: CHINA

China is the third largest country in the world after Russia and Canada, and it's almost the same size as Europe. About one fifth of the world's people live in China, which means that more people live there than in any other country.

'I will thank the Lord very much. I will praise him in front of many people. He defends the helpless. He saved me from those who accuse me.'
Psalm 109: 30–31

MISSIONARIES

In 1950 missionaries had to leave China when it became a communist country. The communists wanted to get rid of all religions in China. The Christians then went through terrible persecution and suffering which some still go through today. However, many have stood strong and firm in their relationship with Jesus and many more people have given their lives to him. Praise God for the huge growth of the church which went from 2.7 million evangelical Christians in 1975 to 75 million in 2010! That means that today about 8% of China's population are now Christians.

NEW WORDS: ★ Communism – a form of government that believes private ownership should be abolished. ★ Evangelical Christians – Christians who take the Bible seriously and believe in Jesus Christ as Saviour and Lord.

PRAY:

- Thank God for the millions of Chinese who know Jesus as their Friend and for the many who are willing to share God's love with others despite being persecuted.

- For the enormous need of printing and distributing Bibles.

DID YOU KNOW? There are so many people in China that in 1979 the government introduced a law limiting each family to only one child!

FACT FILE: Population: 1 billion 331 million
Main Religion: Non-religious

Capital: Beijing (Peking)
Official Language:
Putonghua (Mandarin Chinese)

ON THE MAP

Flag of China

DAY 4: FULANI

The Fulani people [or the Fulbe as they call themselves] are the largest nomadic people group in the world. They are spread across about 20 different countries in West Africa.

It is difficult to know how many Fulani people there are, as many move from one place to another, wandering across desert and land. It is estimated there are between 18-35 million.

They are easy to recognise as they are taller, slimmer and lighter skinned than many of their African neighbours. They are often referred to as 'white' by other Africans because of their lighter skin. Both men and women have markings on their faces around their eyes and mouths which they were given as children.

UNREACHED

The Fulani are united by their language and religion. They are strong Muslims and have helped to spread Islam in West Africa. They say to be Fulani is to be Muslim. They are proud of their religion and are resistant to change. This has made them one of the largest unreached people groups in the world. However, many mission organisations are working to reach them. Through their work, as well as through radio broadcasts and the recently published New Testament in the Fulani language, there is now a growing number of believers.

NEW WORDS: ★ Nomadic – a people who move from place to place.
★ Unreached – a people group that has not been reached with the gospel.

PRAY:

- Praise God for small churches of Fulani believers.

- For more workers, especially those willing to work in isolated places.

DID YOU KNOW? In Fulani culture, a married woman should never say the name of her husband or her first born child!

WORLD CHANGERS The Fulani are one of the largest unreached people groups in the world.

DAY 5: RUSSIA

Russia is the world's largest country. It crosses nine time zones and two continents [Europe and Asia]. It covers more than one eighth of the Earth's habitable land area. Along with China, it neighbours more countries than any other country.

> 'He saw the crowds of people and felt sorry for them because they were worried and helpless. They were like sheep without a shepherd.'
> Matthew 9:36

A trip from Moscow in the West to Vladivostok on the Pacific Ocean takes about nine hours by plane and more than a week by train.

PERSECUTION

Even though Russia is called a Christian nation, you won't meet many who have a personal relationship with Jesus Christ. Millions call themselves Russian Orthodox without actually believing in God. The church in Russia has suffered a lot of persecution over the last 100 years. However, after political changes in Russia about twenty years ago, many missionaries went there and Russians received them with open arms. They had opportunity to tell people about Jesus and to teach the Bible. Churches doubled in number and size. Recently, however, restrictions have gradually been introduced again which are making life difficult for the Christians and churches. There are also few church leaders to help the church to deal with these problems and to lead the way in reaching people for Jesus.

Flag of Russia

PRAY:

- For the millions of Russian Orthodox believers to change to a biblical faith in Jesus.

- For more leaders to lead the churches.

DID YOU KNOW? Russians avoid shaking hands across a doorway as they believe this will bring bad luck!

FACT FILE:

Population: 140 million
Main Religion: Christianity

Capital: Moscow
Official Language: Russian

ON THE MAP

DAY 6: POVERTY

Poverty is still a big problem in the world today. Over one billion people live on less than 70 pence a day or just over a dollar a day. They don't have enough to survive and so they often get sick. One third of deaths in the world every year is caused by poverty.

> 'Being kind to the poor is like lending to the Lord. The Lord will reward you for what you have done.'
> Proverbs 19:17

The poorest countries in the world are found in Africa. There are many verses in the Bible about the poor. We are told to help the poor and those in need. God wants poverty to end and we should want this too. We can pray for the poor asking God to use people to help them. We can also give money to them. We may only be able to give a little but God will increase it like he did in the story about the feeding of the five thousand in the Bible.

MEET BEE AND THE PARKES

HELP THE POOR

The Parkes family sponsored a girl called Bee in Asia. They gave £20 a month which a local Christian project used to help Bee buy food and pay for her schooling. The family, especially their eight year old daughter, prayed for Bee every week. They were delighted to receive letters from Bee saying how well she was doing at school. They read that she had started going to church where she enjoyed praising God.

PRAY:

- For the needs of the poor to be met.

- For the poor to have hope in God.

DID YOU KNOW? An average woman in the UK spends £124 per month on new clothes, shoes and accessories! This amounts to just over $206.

NEW WORDS: ★ Poverty – when someone is extremely poor.
★ Sponsored – when someone is supported financially by another person or organisation

---

WORLD CHANGERS God wants poverty to end and we should want this too.

DAY 7: NORTH KOREA

North Korea is one of the most difficult countries in which to be a Christian. People have to hide their faith; Christian parents can't even share their beliefs with their children until they are old enough to understand the 'dangers'. Owning a Bible could get you killed, or sent to a harsh labour camp.

'We have troubles all around us, but we are not defeated. We do not know what to do, but we do not give up. We are persecuted, but God does not leave us. We are hurt sometimes, but we are not destroyed.'
2 Corinthians 4:8-9

CHRISTIANS ARRESTED

In 2010 hundreds of Christians were arrested. Some were killed, others sentenced to labour camps where they might suffer starvation and sometimes death for their faith. It is estimated that up to 100,000 Christians are currently in prisons or work camps. The government controls the daily life of its poor, hungry people including what they can believe in. It is against the law to be a Christian or take part in any Christian activity. However, despite the risks, there are about 355,000 believers and the Church appears to be growing and standing firm.

DID YOU KNOW? The martial art Taekwondo originated in Korea!

NEW WORDS: ★ Labour camps – places where prisoners are forced to work.

PRAY:

- For strength and comfort to those suffering for Jesus.

- That the government will change its policy and no longer try to destroy the church.

FACT FILE:
Population: 24 million
Main Religion: Non-religious

Capital: Pyongyang
Official Language: Korean

Flag of North Korea

ON THE MAP

DAY 8: MUSLIMS

In the world there are about 1.6 billion Muslims which is about 23% of the world's population. Muslims can be found in almost every country, but mostly in North Africa, the Middle East and Asia.

Muslims worship one god, whom they call Allah, and they believe that Mohammed is their prophet. Muslims believe that they earn God's approval by doing religious things like fasting and that he will judge each person by how many good things and how many bad things they have done.

Their prayers are very different from Christian prayers and have to be said at certain times and in a certain way.

> 'In Christ we are set free by the blood of his death. And so we have forgiveness of sins because of God's rich grace. God gave us that grace fully and freely.'
> Ephesians 1:7-8

JESUS CHRIST

Muslims respect Jesus and believe he is a prophet and healer, but they don't believe he is the Son of God or that he died on the cross and rose again. Muslims do not know that Jesus can forgive us and that we can have a personal relationship with him.

JESUS ROSE FROM THE DEAD

Muslims are normal people, just like you and me, and God loves each of them. It is difficult for Muslims to become Christians as they are often treated badly and rejected by their family and friends.

PRAY:

- That Muslims would not only respect Jesus, but want to know him as their Saviour.

DID YOU KNOW? Ramadan is a special month of prayer and fasting for Muslims. They are not supposed to eat or drink from sunrise to sunset!

NEW WORDS: ★ Prophet– a religious teacher who is believed to be inspired by God.

WORLD CHANGERS Muslims do not know that Jesus can forgive us.

DAY 9: HAITI

Haiti is a country that shares part of an island in the Caribbean. Haiti is in the western third of the island of Hispaniola. The rest of the island is the country Dominican Republic.

It is the poorest country in the western hemisphere and has the highest percentage of orphans. Haiti has huge problems with violence, AIDS, gambling and few people have access to clean water.

'They will pray and obey me…If they do, I will hear them from heaven…and I will heal their land.'
2 Chronicles 7:14

EARTHQUAKE

It was an island largely ignored by the rest of the world until 2010 when a devastating earthquake hit it. About 316,000 people died and over a million were left homeless.

Most Haitians are Roman Catholics but over 75% are involved in Voodoo. Voodoo involves worshipping spirits and often causes people to be fearful and unhappy.

After the 2010 earthquake, many Haitians cried out to God in prayer, asking God to forgive them and asking him for mercy. The president even called for the country to pray and fast for three days. Out of the disaster, God appears to be doing something new among the people of Haiti.

Flag of Haiti

PRAY:

- For God to pour out his Spirit on Haiti as the people cry out to him.

- For God's truth to set people free from Voodoo.

DID YOU KNOW? Haiti was discovered in 1492 by Christopher Columbus!

FACT FILE:
Population: 10 million
Main Religion: Christianity

Capital: Port-au-Prince
Official Language: French

ON THE MAP

DAY 10: TIBETANS

The Tibetan people are an ethnic group who mainly live in a Chinese province called the Tibetan Autonomous Region. The Tibetan plateau is the highest place on earth and is often called 'the roof of the world'. It is surrounded by the beautiful Himalayan and Kun Lun Mountains.

'Lord, there is no god like you. There are no works like yours. Lord, all the nations you have made will come and worship you. They will honour you. You are great, and you do miracles. Only you are God.'
Psalm 86: 8-10

DALAI LAMA

There are about 6 million Tibetans most of whom practice Tibetan Buddhism which has a powerful hold on them. The Dalai Lama is the most important priest and leader of the Tibetan people. They believe that he is a god-king and are devoted to him. Tibet lost its short-lived independence in 1950 when China re-invaded it. This still leads to unrest as the Dalai Lama, who now lives in exile in India, continues to ask for freedom from China's rule.

SMALL CHURCH

The high places of the plateau are known to be very resistant to the gospel. However, there is now a small, but growing number of Tibetan Christians.

NEW WORDS: ★ Plateau – a flat area of high land.

PRAY:

- That Tibetans will see that although the Dalai Lama is their leader and a good man, he is only a man and not a god.

- That they discover that Jesus is the true King of kings and God over all.

DID YOU KNOW? The fat in the milk of an animal called a yak helps the people stay healthy in the extremely cold weather in Tibet!

WORLD CHANGERS There is a small but growing number of Tibetan Christians.

DAY 11: IRAN

Iran is a country in the Middle East that has suffered thirty years of war, hardship and lack of freedom. This has brought a lot of disappointment among people especially the young. This disappointment and frustration have made many open to the gospel and large numbers of people have recently been coming to Jesus. However, Christians in Iran are severely persecuted and are regularly arrested. Some are treated badly in prison while others are released but watched closely.

> 'Since the day we heard this about you, we have continued praying for you … Then God will strengthen you with his own great power. And you will not give up when troubles come.'
> Colossians 1:9 & 11

MEET MARYAM

Maryam and Marzieh are two young Christian women from Iran who used to be Muslims. They were arrested for telling other people about Jesus. They were under great pressure to return to being Muslims again, but both women stood firm and refused to deny their Christian

Flag of Iran

faith. While in prison they were told that many Christians around the world were praying for them. They said that this encouraged and strengthened them. After a year in prison they were eventually allowed to leave and live in another country. Iran and its people need us to continually remember them in our prayers.

NEW WORDS: ★ Persecuted – to be badly treated often because of religion or race.

PRAY:

- Thank God that he is at work amongst the people of Iran.

- That Christians will stand firm in their faith despite the problems they face.

DID YOU KNOW? Iran is surrounded by Afghanistan, Armenia, Azerbaijan, Iraq, Pakistan, Turkey and Turkmenistan.

FACT FILE
Population: 75 million
Main Religion: Islam

Capital: Tehran
Official Language: Persian

ON THE MAP

DAY 12: CHILD LABOUR

One in six children in the world work to make a living. Many of them work in dangerous conditions, such as mines. Some work with dangerous machinery or do heavy work on farms. Some work very long hours.

Can you imagine what it is like for a seven year old girl to have to work twelve hours a day for six days a week? Life only consists of work and sleep.

'Get up, cry out
in the night.
Cry all through
the night. Pour out your heart
like water in prayer to the Lord.
Lift up your hands in prayer to him.
Pray for the life of your children.
They are fainting with hunger
on every street corner.'
Lamentations 2:19

MEET RAKSMEY

Many children in Cambodia work to help their families. Raksmey works in a rubbish dump in Phnom Penh, Cambodia. The rubbish dump is over 100 acres in size. Fires burn all the time, and poisonous fumes rise off the smoke from the fires. The rubbish dump also has high levels of a chemical that causes cancer. Raksmey comes here almost every day, working without shoes or a shirt to look through the rubbish to find things he can sell.

'I know it is difficult work, but I need to help my family,' he says.

PRAY FOR THE POOR

PRAY:

- That God would keep the children safe and that they wouldn't have to work.

- That the children would hear about Jesus and have hope in him.

DID YOU KNOW? Some children in India work in clothing factories for just 60 pence per day or 99 cents!

WORLD CHANGERS
One in six children in the world work to make a living.

DAY 13: INDIA

India is a country with a million gods and a billion people! Indians are very religious. Most of them are Hindus who believe and worship many different gods. They hope that offering food, money or prayers will bring peace and protection from evil spirits. They also believe that washing in the River Ganges will wash away their sin.

'I am the only good God. I am the Saviour. .. All people everywhere follow me and be saved. I am God. There is no other God.'
Isaiah 45:21–22

Millions of people in India are affected by poverty. Some are homeless, blind and sick. Some children are orphans or were abandoned and live on the streets. There is a lot of need throughout the country.

PEOPLE GROUPS

India is the most mixed nation in the world with over 2,500 people groups and 456 languages. Christian missionaries have worked in India for many years but now few of them can get visas to work there. However, there are thousands of Indian missionaries and Christians who are bravely talking to their own people about Jesus. Some have been attacked for doing this. Thousands of churches have been planted and yet the challenge remains: 903 million Hindus, 172 million Muslims and 23 million Sikhs who have not heard about Jesus!

Flag of India

NEW WORDS: ★ People group – people sharing the same language and way of living.

PRAY:

- That Indians will believe in the one and only God who loves them.

- Thank God for Indians prepared to tell others about Jesus.

DID YOU KNOW? Over 17% of the world's population are Indian!

FACT FILE:
Population: 1 billion 214 million
Main Religion: Hinduism

Capital: Delhi
Official Language: Hindi

ON THE MAP

DAY 14: CLEAN WATER

One in eight people in the world don't have toilets or clean water nearby. This causes over 3.4 million people to die each year from water-related diseases. This is over 9,000 deaths per day.

'Every person who drinks this water will be thirsty again. But whoever drinks the water I give will never be thirsty again. The water I give will become a spring of water flowing inside him. It will give him eternal life.'
John 4:13-14

TANZANIA

Nakwetikya from Tanzania, used to collect water mixed with animal and human waste from a deep pit. Sickness and deaths were common but this changed with the WaterAid project.

'The situation here used to be bleak,' she explains. 'There was no water and we had to dig pits to find some. Can you imagine what it was like? My legs used to shake with fear before climbing down those holes. There was no choice. If I didn't get water, my family couldn't eat, wash or even have a drink.

When I heard that we were going to get clean water, I remember laughing. I can only compare it to someone who is in prison for a long time. When they are set free it's the most fantastic experience.'

DID YOU KNOW? When you brush your teeth, turn the tap off as you can save up to 225 litres a week!

PRAY

- For organisations who help people by building hand pumps and toilets.

- That when the need for clean water has been met, the people would then have a thirst to know God.

GET INTO IT

Throughout your day, from the moment you get up until you go to bed at night, work out how many times you use water. In a notebook write down everything you drink, all the times you wash, or someone washes something for you. Don't forget the different machines that use water such as washing machines. Then remember to thank God for this wonderful gift.

WORLD CHANGERS

DID YOU KNOW? WaterAid is an international non-profit organisation that works in 27 countries transforming millions of lives with clean water, safe toilets and hygiene education.

DAY 15: CAMBODIA

Cambodia is one of the poorest countries in Asia. It went through great suffering in the 1970s during the reign of Pol Pot and the Khmer Rouge. Nearly two million people were killed and many were injured by landmines.

Most Cambodians over the age of thirty need deep healing from their losses and suffering. Some have found God who has brought healing and hope to their lives.

'He was wounded
for the wrong things
we did...and we are
healed because of his wounds.'
Isaiah 53:5

MEET ADDHEKA

Addheka was thirteen years old when the Khmer Rouge took control of the country. Her mother had a job working for them as the head of investigation, and so she had many books including Christian stories at home. One particular Christian book challenged Addheka to accept Jesus as her Saviour. During the war, Addheka's parents

Flag of Cambodia

and many other family members died of hunger but Addheka slept in fields and survived. Soldiers were told to kill her on three different occasions but each time God delivered her.

Now many years later, Addheka has committed her life to serve Jesus. She works to help the poor to be able to go to school and encourages them to accept Jesus as their Saviour as she did long ago.

PRAY:

- For Cambodians to find hope and healing in God.

- For the government to seek the best for the country.

DID YOU KNOW? The world's largest religious building called the Angkor Wat is in Cambodia. It is pictured on their flag!

FACT FILE

Population: 15 million
Main Religion: Buddhism

Capital: Phnom Penh
Official Language: Khmer

ON THE MAP

DAY 16: RADIO

Telling people about Jesus through the radio is a great way to reach people around the world in their own language. Some people live in countries where it's difficult to hear about Christianity. This is often because of persecution, because they can't read or write, because they don't have a Bible or because they live in remote areas where missionaries cannot go. Radio is often their only way to hear about Jesus.

'But before people can trust in the Lord for help, they must believe in him. And before they can believe in the Lord, they must hear about him. And for them to hear about the Lord someone must tell them.'
Romans 10:14

A RADIO CHURCH

A Christian radio station once received a letter from a listener in China who was a Christian. After the listener had retired, he spent a lot of time in study and prayer and eventually became an evangelist. In his travels throughout China he came across an isolated village of 100 people. There were no roads in or out of the village. The evangelist started talking to a man in the village and shared with him about Jesus. It was not long before the villager responded and said, 'We know all about Jesus. We have a radio here and we've been listening to Christian broadcasts for a long time. We even have a church with thirty five members.' The evangelist was amazed at how God had used radio to form a church.

TELL PEOPLE ABOUT JESUS

PRAY:

- That people who listen to Christian radio around the world would respond to God's message of love and hope.

DID YOU KNOW? An AM radio wave is as long as a football field!

NEW WORDS: Evangelist – a person who tries to convert others to the Christian faith.

GET INTO IT

Listen to a Christian broadcast on the radio or online. Take some notes about the music and stories you listen to.

Make a radio broadcast of your own. You could record this or perform it live to friends and family. Use the information in this book as the basis for your programme.

Perhaps you could perform at your youth group? You could even raise funds for missions!

DAY 17: MEXICO

Mexico is the largest Spanish-speaking country in the world. It is a country in Central America that is located in the 'Ring of Fire' which is one of the Earth's most violent earthquake and volcano areas. It therefore has a history of many destructive earthquakes. A series of earthquakes in 1985 killed at least 10,000 people and caused major damage to Mexico City. These natural disasters as well as poverty, drugs and gang violence cause a lot of problems in the country.

'Shout to the Lord, all the earth. Serve the Lord with joy. Come before him with singing. Know that the Lord is God.'
Psalm 100:1–3

Mexico has the world's second highest number of Roman Catholics. Most Mexicans are Roman Catholics but not everyone practises their beliefs. Some even mix it with beliefs about ancient gods and the spirit world.

A REASON TO CELEBRATE

Praise God, however, that the church is growing quickly in Mexico. Now 8% of the population are evangelical Christians. Mexicans love to have fun and celebrate. Those who come to know Jesus have a new reason to do so. They are eager to share their faith and are reaching out to those around them. There are even some Christians who are being sent out from Mexico to other countries as missionaries.

Flag of Mexico

PRAY:

- For Mexico City where 19 million people live but there are few churches.

- For God to use Mexicans to reach out to people around them and in other countries.

DID YOU KNOW? Mexico introduced chocolate to the world…yum!

FACT FILE:
Population: 111 million
Main Religion: Christianity

Capital: Mexico City
Official Language: Spanish

ON THE MAP

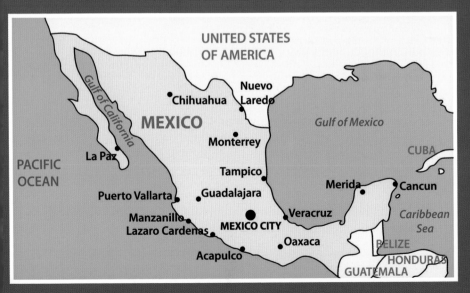

DAY 18: PRISONERS

There are people in prisons for many different reasons; some for a long time and some for a short time. There are opportunities for Christians to share with prisoners throughout the world about Jesus. Through evangelism in prisons, many have become Christians and now know the freedom and hope that they can have in God.

'I was in prison, and you visited me. Then the good people will answer…"When did we see you sick or in prison and care for you?" Then the King will answer, "I tell you the truth. Anything you did for any of my people here, you also did for me."'
Matthew 25:36-37, 39-40

MEET ALAN

Alan, a missionary in Thailand, visits people in prison in Bangkok. He talks to them about Jesus and takes them small gifts. One year at a Christmas outreach at the prison, a young man named Ooi listened to the message about Jesus. He then started going to the weekly Christian group in the prison where he gave his life to the Lord and was completely changed. He used to have a problem with anger but he testifies to how God has dealt with this. Recently another prisoner spat on him, but instead of getting angry and violent like he used to do, Ooi said, 'I forgive you for doing that. God loves you'. He then prayed for the man.

NEW WORDS: ★ Evangelism – to spread the Christian gospel by preaching or personal witness.

PRAY:

- For prisoners throughout the world to experience God's love and the freedom that they can have in him.

DID YOU KNOW? There are over 10 million prisoners in the world and the United States has more than any other country!

WORLD CHANGERS Through evangelism in prisons many have become Christians.

DAY 19: TURKEY

Turkey is a country that is located in two continents. Three percent is in Europe and the other 97 percent is in Asia. It is torn between the East and the West, and divided on many issues.

'No servant can serve two masters. He will hate one master and love the other. Or he will follow one master and refuse to follow the other. You cannot serve both God and money.'
Luke 16:13

Turkey has a Christian history. Paul lived in Tarsus and the seven churches in the book of Revelation are all in Turkey. Now it is 97% Muslim and is said to be the largest unreached country in the world. It is also said to have more mosques [where Muslims pray and worship] per person than any other country.

STEADY INCREASE

However, there is now a slow but steady increase in the number of Christians. About 50 years ago, there were probably only about ten Turkish or Kurdish believers but by 2010 there were around 4,000. It isn't easy for Turks who follow Jesus to tell others about him. The law doesn't say that people can't become Christians but some have been prevented from meeting together to worship God. Others have lost their jobs or been put in prison.

Flag of Turkey

PRAY:

- For more Turks to choose to follow Jesus.

- For Turkish Christians to be strong in difficult times.

DID YOU KNOW? Noah's ark landed on Mount Ararat, which is in Turkey!

FACT FILE:
Population: 76 million
Main Religion: Islam

Capital: Ankara
Official Language: Turkish

ON THE MAP

DAY 20: STREET KIDS

Throughout the world especially in South America and Asia, millions of children don't live in homes. They live in cardboard boxes, empty buildings, parks or on the streets. They are forced to live on the streets without the safety of a family home. It is very dangerous for them.

'But Jesus said, "Let the little children come to me. Don't stop them, because the kingdom of heaven belongs to people who are like these children."' Matthew 19:14

Some are there because they are orphans or have been abandoned; some have run away from home because of family breakdown; some are there because of poverty and some because of overcrowding in cities.

Many street children have to work on the streets selling things or begging. According to the United Nations there are around 100 million children who live or work on the streets.

MEET MICHLA

CHILDREN CAN COME TO JESUS

Michla, age 12 from Haiti says, 'I've been on the streets for four years. I make my living by washing cars and loading them up or sometimes begging. I'm not living with my parents because they told me to leave a long time ago, then they moved away somewhere and disappeared. They have many other kids and said they could not afford me. They said I should be able to make my own living without bothering them.'

PRAY:

- For safety and protection of street children.

- That they would know Jesus as their friend who is always with them.

DID YOU KNOW? In many countries street children are given unkind names. Columbian street children are called 'bed bugs', in Rwanda 'dirty kids' and in Brazil, 'little criminals'!

WORLD CHANGERS There are around 100 million children who live on the streets.

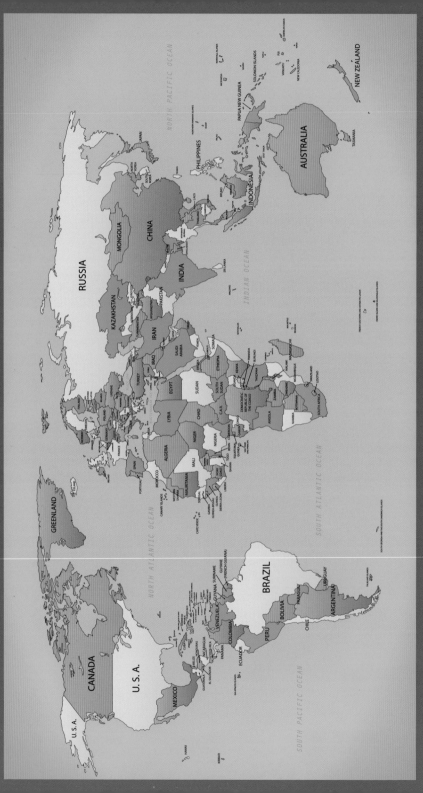

MAP OF THE WORLD

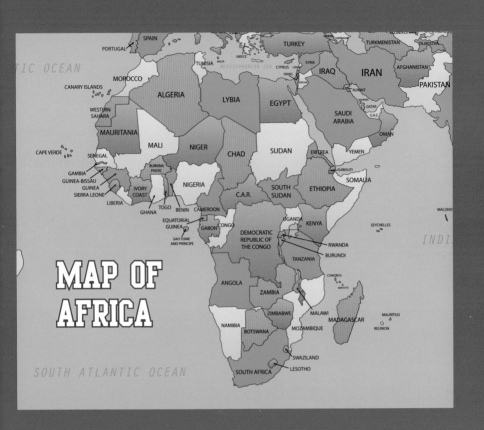

MAP OF AFRICA

MAP OF EUROPE AND ASIA

DAY 21: MONGOLIA

Mongolia is a country of mountains and desert and is found between Russia and China. It was a communist country for many years, but in 1990 it changed and then people were allowed to choose which religion they wanted to follow.

In 1989 there may have been only four Mongolian Christians. Today, there are over 40,000 believers in hundreds of churches and groups, meeting in most parts of the country!

'We will tell those who come later about the praises of the Lord. We will tell about his power and the miracles he has done.'
Psalm 78:4

MEET BAT-ERDENE

In 1991, a music teacher called Bat-Erdene went to church with a friend for the first time. The church asked him to accompany them in their singing because he was a musician and so he started going to church every week. Bat-Erdene eventually gave his life to God and was one of many in a movement of God drawing young people to Jesus. He is now a pastor and a principal of a Bible college.

It is good that Mongolian churches have grown, but unfortunately few children are brought to church. The next generation needs to hear about God too.

Flag of Mongolia

PRAY:

- Praise God for the many Mongolian Christians who have come to know him over the last twenty years.

- For children to be brought to church and become the next generation of Mongolian believers.

DID YOU KNOW? Most Mongolians learn to ride a horse almost as soon as they learn to walk!

FACT FILE:
Population: 3 million
Main Religion: Buddhism and Shamanism

Capital: Ulaanbaatar [Ulan Bator]
Official Language: Khalkha Mongolian

ON THE MAP

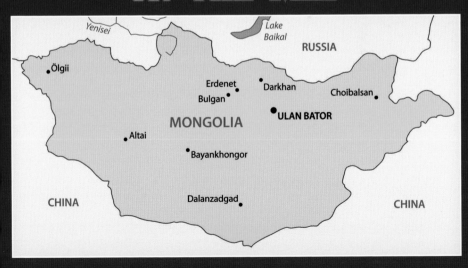

DAY 22: BUDDHISTS

There are about 478 million Buddhists in the world which is about 7% of the world's population. Most Buddhists live in Asia in countries such as China, Japan, Thailand, Vietnam and Myanmar.

> 'Grace and peace be given to you more and more. You will have grace and peace because you truly know God and Jesus our Lord.'
> 2 Peter 1:2

Buddhism is a religion that was founded by a man called Siddharta Gautama who lived about 2,500 years ago. His followers called him the Buddha, which means the 'enlightened one'. Buddhists believe that after they die they are reborn as another person or even an animal.

They believe that if they do good things in this life, they will earn a better life when they are reborn. Buddhists often pray, meditate and chant religious texts. They worship at ornate temples where monks live, or at a shrine at home. Flowers, candles and incense are made as offerings when they worship.

MEET CHAY

Chay was a Buddhist who was trying to reach Nirvana, which is peace and freedom from suffering and the cycle of rebirth. One day a missionary asked Chay if he prayed and what he prayed for. Chay answered that he often prayed to Buddha for peace. The missionary told Chay about the peace that he himself had received from Jesus. Chay didn't have any peace regardless of praying and meditating and so wanted to know more. As he heard more about Jesus and the hope of eternal life, he decided to give his life to God.

PRAY:

- For Buddhists to find peace and hope in God.

NEW WORDS: ★ Meditate – to think deeply and quietly.

DID YOU KNOW? Buddhists often go to temples on a day with a full moon!

WORLD CHANGERS There are 478 million Buddhists in the world.

DAY 23: BURKINA FASO

Burkina Faso is a country in West Africa which often suffers from drought and famine. It is one of the poorest countries in the world.

Despite life being difficult in Burkina Faso, God has been at work in the country over several decades. There has been an increase in evangelical Christians from 10,000 in 1960 to 1.44 million in 2010. There are seventy-eight different people groups in Burkina Faso and many of them still live in fear of evil spirits.

'Jesus became like men and died so that He could free them. They were like slaves all their lives because of their fear of death.'
Hebrews 2:15

MEET SIE

Sie was a little boy living in a remote village in Burkina Faso. He was very ill with malaria and so his mum in desperation went to get help from the local witch doctor. The witch doctor killed a chicken as he believed it would please the evil spirits he thought were making Sie ill. Sie's Mum then tied an amulet around his neck as she felt it would protect him from further attacks by evil spirits.

Flag of Burkino Faso

People like Sie's family, who don't know Jesus, are living in fear and need to hear about God who can set them free.

> **NEW WORDS:** ★ People group – people sharing the same language and way of living.

PRAY:

- For people in Burkina Faso to hear about Jesus who can set them free.

- For more missionaries to go and tell them about Jesus.

DID YOU KNOW? An amulet is a 'charm' usually made of sticks, bones or feathers which the wearers believe will protect them from sickness and harm!

FACT FILE:
Population: 16 million
Main Religion: Islam

Capital: Ouagadougou
Official Language: French

ON THE MAP

DAY 24: NEIGHBOURS

We are told in the Bible to share our faith with other people. This means it is our responsibility to tell our neighbours and people in our town about Jesus.

We don't have to be living in another country to do the work of a missionary. There are people living near us or at our school or work place who don't know Jesus.

'But the Holy Spirit will come to you. Then you will receive power. You will be my witnesses – in Jerusalem, in all of Judea, in Samaria, and in every part of the world.'
Acts 1:8

MEET CLAIRE

A girl called Claire was only ten years old when she decided that she wanted to tell her friends about Jesus. She was very nervous and didn't know what to say. She prayed with her mum about it and then eventually invited her friends to her church that Sunday. Claire was delighted that one of her friends, Emma, came to church. Emma really enjoyed it and said that everyone was so nice, and different from other people whom she knew. She carried on going to church and hearing about God. Claire was amazed at how easy it had been to invite her friend. She knew it was because Jesus had helped her to be bold and to know what to say.

SHARE YOUR FAITH

PRAY:

- For your neighbours and friends at school, college or work.

DID YOU KNOW? Research shows that the best way to share the Christian faith is through 'friendship evangelism'. This is simply telling your neighbours and friends about Jesus!

GET INTO IT

How many words [2 letters or more] can you make out of the word, 'neighbours'?

Under 3 words – poor

4-6 words – average

7-12 words – good

12+ words – excellent

DAY 25: KAZAKHSTAN

Kazakhstan is big! It is the world's ninth-largest country and stretches from the Caspian Sea (an inland sea) in the west to China in the east. It is the largest landlocked country in the world and is located in two continents, Asia and Europe.

'The Lord's name should be praised from where the sun rises to where it sets. The Lord is supreme over all the nations. His glory reaches to the skies.'
Psalm 113:3-4

Kazakhstan has gone through a lot of change. The people used to be nomads who never lived in one place for very long but travelled across the land with their animals. Their homes used to be felt tents but now many live in apartment blocks and are well-educated. Almost all Kazakhs see themselves as Muslims, but most of them don't practise their religion and superstition is strong. In 1991 Kazakhstan became independent from the Soviet Union. There was a great openness to the gospel after this and many became Christians. The Kazakh Church is now growing – from almost no Kazakh believers in 1990 to about 15,000 in 2010!

Christians are telling Kazakhs about God's love and about how they don't have to be afraid if they ask Jesus to protect them. The challenge is now to see the other 99.9 % of Kazakhs reached with the gospel.

Flag of Kazakhstan

PRAY:

- Praise God for Kazakhs becoming Christians.

- For the big demand for Bibles especially for the Kazakh New Testament.

DID YOU KNOW? There are more horses in Kazakhstan than women!

FACT FILE:
Population: 16 million
Main Religion: Islam

Capital: Astana
Official Language: Kazakh

ON THE MAP

DAY 26: WAR

Some countries in the world today are at war with other countries. Some countries are involved in a civil war where groups of people within a country fight each other.

> 'You will hear about wars and stories of wars that are coming. But don't be afraid. These things must happen before the end comes. Nations will fight against nations. Kingdoms will fight against other kingdoms.'
> Matthew 24:6–7

Wars can start for a variety of reasons. Sometimes it is because of a fight over land, money or power.

Unfortunately many innocent people including children are affected by war. Some have to leave their homes to live somewhere safer and many are injured or killed. Wars often disrupt school and can make people poorer.

MEET SANA

Sana is a nine year old girl who was living in Syria. Due to civil war in Syria many people have suffered. One day a rocket fell on Sana's house. No one was injured but her family decided they had to escape the violence all around them. They fled to Jordan which is a country next to Syria. They are now living in a tent in a refugee camp where life is very hard for them. They are however more fortunate than some other families who have experienced someone in their family being killed.

DON'T BE AFRAID

PRAY

- Thank God for peace where you live.

- For there to be peace in countries at war.

- For innocent people affected by war to have hope in God.

DID YOU KNOW? It is recorded that the most peaceful country in the world today is Iceland!

WORLD CHANGERS

Many innocent people are affected by war.

DAY 27: THE U.S.A.

The United States of America [USA] is also called the United States [US] or sometimes America. It is the fourth largest country in the world by land area and the third largest by population.

'You should pray for kings and for all who have authority. Pray for the leaders so that we can have quiet and peaceful lives - lives full of worship and respect for God...God wants all people to be saved. And he wants everyone to know the truth.'
I Timothy 2:2 & 4

The US is one of the most diverse countries in the world with people from many different countries such as Mexico, China and the Philippines living there. About 13% of the population use a language other than English at home.

The US has a strong Christian history. From its early days until now, no other country has been so strongly influenced by Christianity. Almost a third of the population are evangelical Christians. However, the country still has many problems in society and large numbers don't know Jesus. Billy Graham, the world famous American evangelist, who has been a spiritual advisor to presidents of the US, recently said that the country has turned its back on God and its Christian foundations but says that it isn't too late.

Flag of the U.S.A.

God wants Americans from all backgrounds and races to be saved. He wants us to pray for the leaders of countries. Let us pray for the president and leaders of the US to influence their country and the rest of the world in a godly way.

PRAY:

- For American Christians to speak the truth in love to those who don't know God.

- For the leaders of the US to influence their country and the world for good.

DID YOU KNOW? The US is made up of 50 states which are represented by the 50 stars on the American flag!

FACT FILE:
Population: 318 million
Main religion: Christianity

Capital: Washington,DC
Official language: English

ON THE MAP

DAY 28: THE INTERNET

There are about 2.4 billion people who use the Internet. That is over a third of the world's population. Some people use search engines on computers to find all kinds of information from news to music. Some search to learn more about God. 'Is there a God?' is a question often asked into cyberspace.

'Pray that God will give us an opportunity to tell people his message. Pray that we can preach the secret truth that God has made known about Christ.'
Colossians 4:3

The Internet is a unique way to tell people about God, especially young people.

Websites, chat rooms, email and messaging are all tools that can be used. It is an open door of opportunity to reach people.

MEET BURAK

Burak is a young Turk who was searching for information about Jesus on the internet. He first found a Christian website on Facebook, and went on to connect with believers via other Christian websites too. After receiving a Bible and other materials, he was eager to meet up with a Christian. Burak went to a Christmas party hosted by the Christian website and was then connected to a local church where he has been attending ever since. There are many young men and women in different countries making similar journeys. Some are giving their lives to Jesus.

REACH PEOPLE

PRAY:

- That more people who visit Christian websites will come to faith in Jesus.

NEW WORDS: ★ Search engine – a computer programme that helps you search for something on the Internet. ★ Cyberspace – the online world of computer networks and the Internet.

WORLD CHANGERS The Internet is a unique way to tell people about God.

DAY 29: JAPAN

Japan is made up of four large islands and about 3,000 smaller ones. It is a land of contrasts from beautiful mountains to skyscraper buildings in the cities. It is a wealthy and powerful country that influences the world. This doesn't make us think of it as a normal country where missionaries work and yet few people who live there have ever heard of Jesus as a Saviour.

'Do not change yourselves to be like the people of this world. But be changed within by a new way of thinking. Then you will be able to decide what God wants for you. And you will be able to know what is good and pleasing to God and what is perfect.'
Romans 12:2

The Japanese people are polite and very hard-working but can often be too busy to take notice of the gospel. They have a lot of pressure to follow Buddhist and Shinto practices and to conform to what everyone else in Japan does and to what is expected of them. The pressure to be like other people and the need to be successful in their work squeezes out Christianity, particularly for Japanese men. However, there are reports that many Japanese are now becoming fed up with the emptiness of their lifestyles.

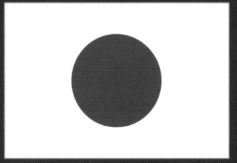

Flag of Japan

PRAY:

- For the Japanese to have strength to follow God and not feel the need to be like others.

- For more Japanese men to become Christians.

DID YOU KNOW? Japan has over 100 active volcanoes, which is more than any other country!

FACT FILE:
Population: 127 million
Main Religion: Buddhism/Shintoism

Capital: Tokyo-Yokohama
Official Language: Japanese

ON THE MAP

DAY 30: MALARIA

Malaria is a disease that you get through the bite of an infected insect called a mosquito. It can cause people to be very sick or to die.

Mosquitoes are the deadliest killers on earth. More people die from their bite than from any other insect or animal on our planet.

Mosquitoes carry a number of deadly diseases but the most deadly is malaria, especially in Africa. Every year around a million people die from malaria, many of whom are children.

'When birds are sold, two small birds cost only a penny. But not even one of the little birds can die without your Father's knowing it. God even knows how many hairs are on your head. So don't be afraid. You are worth much more than many birds.'
Matthew 10:29-31

MEET MUMU

Malaria can be prevented by using a mosquito net. However, a lot of people can't afford to buy one. Mumu, a child in Kenya, is no stranger to malaria. Several times a year she struggled through the fever, headaches and pain of malaria. Then Mumu, along with more than 400 children in her community, received a treated mosquito bed net from the Christian organisation, Compassion. "Now I sleep comfortably," she says. "I do my homework without even thinking about the mosquitoes. I am glad that I have a net to sleep under every night!"

God cares about Mumu and every other person who is affected by malaria.

PRAY:

- For protection of people who live in areas where there is malaria.

- For more mosquito nets to be given to people who need them.

DID YOU KNOW? Only female mosquitoes bite people!

WORLD CHANGERS Every year around a million people die from malaria.

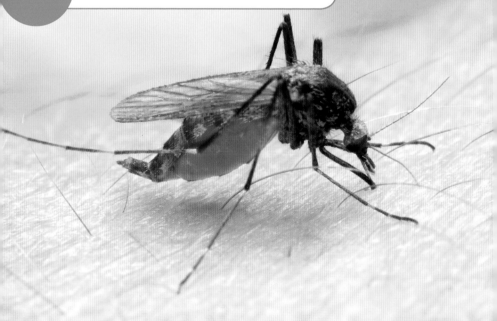

DAY 31: ALBANIA

Albania is a mountainous country which is just 45 miles across the Strait of Otranto from Italy. It is one of Europe's two poorest countries.

It is known for being the home of Mother Teresa, who showed great compassion by helping the poor and sick in the streets of Calcutta in India.

'And I will build my church on this rock. The power of death will not be able to defeat my church.'
Matthew 16:18

Albania used to be a communist country and no religion was allowed. However, in the 1990s the country changed after people had been praying for it for many years. Missionaries could then go into the country and tell people about Jesus. Since then the number of evangelical Christians has grown from nearly zero to several thousands. The church is growing in Albania despite it being one of the only majority Muslim countries in Europe.

In 2012 there was a massive evangelistic event in the capital of Albania supported by the churches in the city. More than 20,000 people were attracted to the two day event which included live music and different stalls. An evangelist called Luis Palau preached the good news of Jesus Christ and over 2,300 people made decisions to follow Christ.

THE CHURCH IS GROWING

Flag of Albania

PRAY:

- For Albanian Muslims to meet the living Christ.

- For the church to continue to grow.

FACT FILE:

Population: 3 million
Main Religion: Islam

Capital: Tirana
Official Language: Albanian

DID YOU KNOW?

In Albania, nodding the head means 'no', and shaking the head means 'yes'!

ON THE MAP

DAY 32: STUDENTS

In most countries throughout the world, there are millions of students. Universities and colleges are great places where students can learn. However, they are also places where students can experience debt, loneliness and pressure. Very few students these days have a Christian faith, and so there is a big opportunity to share the good news of Jesus with them as many are open to Christianity.

'You are young, but do not let anyone treat you as if you were not important. Be an example to show the believers how they should live.'
I Timothy 4:12

MEET JOHN

John was a student at a university in England. He had been looking forward to being independent and studying at university for a long time but it wasn't what he expected. He struggled with money and missed home. He went out to parties with other students but still felt lonely inside and often found himself feeling desperate and wondering what life was all about. It was at this time that another student invited him to the Christian Union. At the Christian Union he found everyone friendly and saw that they had something that he was missing in his life. He saw that they had peace and a personal relationship with Jesus. This was the first time that John had heard about Christianity and after a while he gave his life to God.

SHARE THE GOOD NEWS

PRAY:

- For Christian students to reach out with God's love to other students.

- For countries with universities where there is no Christian witness.

DID YOU KNOW? In the U.K. 1974 was the year of the last all-male college in Oxford and Magdalene College, Cambridge didn't admit women until 1988!

NEW WORDS: ★ Debt – something that you owe someone, for example, money.

WORLD CHANGERS Very few students have a Christian faith.

DAY 33: YEMEN

Yemen is a country in the Middle East that borders Saudi Arabia and Oman. About three thousand years ago, the Queen of Sheba [I Kings 10] reigned in what is now the land of Yemen. She exchanged gifts with King Solomon and asked him for wisdom. However, over 1,500 years after the Queen lived, Yemen became a Muslim country.

'People will come from Sheba bringing gold and incense. And they will sing praises to the Lord.'
Isaiah 60:6

It is the poorest country in the Arab world and over the last 40 years it has suffered three civil wars as well as conflicts with neighbouring countries.

Yemen is now one of the world's least evangelised countries, with one of the youngest and fastest growing populations.

Christians have tried to tell people in Yemen about Jesus. It's hard because Muslims are proud of their religion and all Yemenis are expected to be Muslims. Because families are very close, it is very difficult for one member of the family to choose another religion. Such a person could be considered a traitor who deserves to die.

Despite these difficult circumstances, some people are finding life in Jesus especially through radio broadcasts and Bible distribution.

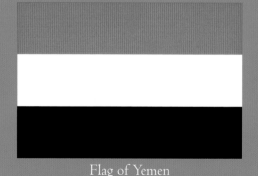

Flag of Yemen

74

PRAY:

- That the modern people of Sheba would seek after God's wisdom as promised in the book of Isaiah.

- For whole families to know Jesus.

> **DID YOU KNOW?** Yemen's most important export used to be frankincense but it is now oil!

FACT FILE:
Population: 24 million
Main Religion: Islam

Capital: Sana'a
Official Language: Arabic

ON THE MAP

LIFE IN JESUS

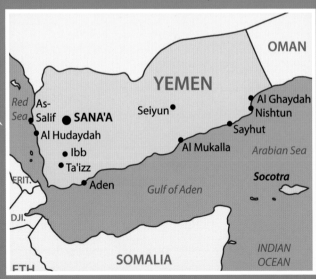

DAY 34: REFUGEES

As you sit in your own comfortable house, can you imagine what it would be like to be a refugee, having to flee from your home and country, hoping to find a place where you could feel safe?

'Jesus said to him, "The foxes have holes to live in. The birds have nests to live in. But the Son of Man has no place where he can rest his head."'
Matthew 8:20

There are about 43 million refugees in the world and most of them are women and children. Refugees are frightened to stay in their own homes because of persecution, war or natural disaster. They leave everything behind and try to find a new life. Some have had to leave their homes and villages to find a place to live in another part of their own country or in a different country altogether.

MYANMAR REFUGEES

There are people living in refugee camps on the Thai/Myanmar border who were born there, educated there, married there and have children who were born there. That is two generations of families who have never known freedom. Myanmar refugees are not allowed outside the camps and opportunities to earn a living are very limited. With no electricity, no phones and no Internet, it's a life cut off from the outside world.

> IMAGINE BEING A REFUGEE

PRAY:

- That refugees would know God's love and find hope in him for each day.

- That they would find security in a relationship with Jesus.

DID YOU KNOW? Jesus was a refugee. His family fled from Israel because of King Herod!

WORLD CHANGERS There are about 43 million refugees in the world.

DAY 35: THAILAND

Thailand is a country in the continent of Asia where most people are Buddhists. They believe that if they do good things in this life, they will earn a better life when they are reborn.

One day a teenager in Thailand called Awm left home and went to college with tears streaming down her face. Her parents wanted her to go to the temple with them to make merit but she didn't want to go now that she was a Christian.

'That is why you need to put on God's full armour. Then on the day of evil you will be able to stand strong. And when you have finished the whole fight, you will still be standing.'
Ephesians 6:13

Awm had become a Christian at an English camp where some missionaries had told her about God. She now loved Jesus and wanted to follow him, however she had been taught to respect and obey her parents. They pressured her time and time again to make merit, worship idols or wear spirit strings around her wrists again. They were scared that something bad would happen to her if she didn't follow their beliefs. They said that she should do it out of respect for her family, especially her elderly grandparents. They didn't seem to understand that she wasn't a Buddhist anymore. Like many other Thai people, they repeated the saying, 'To be Thai is to be Buddhist', and they said that Christianity was just for foreigners.

NEW WORDS: ★ Make merit – when Buddhists do good things believing it will bring happiness and peace after death.

PRAY:

- For young people in Thailand to stand strong in God.

- For whole families to become Christians.

DID YOU KNOW? The King of Thailand is the longest reigning monarch in the world!

FACT FILE:
Population: 68 million
Main Religion: Buddhism

Capital: Bangkok
Official Language: Thai

ON THE MAP

Flag of Thailand

BURMA
LAOS
Chiang Mai
Lampang
Udon Thani
Phitsanulok
Khon Kaen
THAILAND
Nakhon Sawan
Nakhon Ratchasima
Ubon Ratchathani
Kanchanaburi
BANGKOK
Chonburi
Andaman Sea
Pattaya
Rayong
Ko Chang
CAMBODIA
Prachuap Khin Khan
Gulf of Thailand
VIETNAM
Surat Thani
Nakhon Si Thammarat
Krabi
South China Sea
Phuket
MALAYSIA

DO YOU LOVE JESUS?

79

DAY 36: 10/40 WINDOW

The 10/40 Window is a rectangular-shaped area of the world extending from West Africa to East Asia, from ten degrees south to forty degrees north of the Equator.

Two thirds of the world's population live in the 68 countries that it covers.

It is home to the majority of the world's poor and is an area where people suffer from terrible poverty, famine and diseases.

'The devil who rules this world has blinded the minds of those who do not believe. They cannot see the light of the Good News — the Good News about the glory of Christ, who is exactly like God.'
2 Corinthians 4:4

The 10/40 Window contains the most non-Christians in the world with about 90% of the world's unreached living in the area. Most major non-Christian religions are based there, such as Islam, Hinduism and Buddhism. About 1.6 billion of people living there have never had the chance to hear the gospel of Jesus Christ - not even once!

Many Christians there suffer awful persecution. Forty five of the fifty worst countries in the world for persecution of Christians are in the 10/40 Window.

There needs to be a breakthrough in this area for people to see the light of the good news about Jesus.

NEW WORDS: ★ Equator – an imaginary circle around the earth, an equal distance from the North and South Poles.

PRAY:

- That there would be a breakthrough in the 10/40 Window with many people coming to know Jesus.

- For the Christians who live there and suffer persecution.

THE 10/40 WINDOW

DID YOU KNOW? The Equator is about 25 thousand miles long and runs through 13 countries including Brazil, India and Kenya. It is usually very hot and rainy near the Equator!

DAY 37: SENEGAL

Senegal is a country in the west of Africa. It is one of the most stable countries in the continent. It is also one of the few countries with a large Muslim majority but where missionary work can be done freely. It is an open country where missionaries have been working for over 120 years. However, despite all of this, there are still very few Senegalese who are followers of Jesus.

'I am the Lord. I am the God of every person on the earth. You know that nothing is impossible for me.' Jeremiah 32:27

There are many different people groups in Senegal such as the Wolof, Fulani and Mande, but they also remain almost completely Muslim too. Dakar, the capital of Senegal, is home to over a quarter of the population and has representatives of every ethnic group. It is a key place to reach people.

REACH THE 95

The missionaries in Senegal are continuing to trust God for a breakthrough. They are praying to 'reach the 95'. This means reaching 95% of the 13 million population who are Muslim and don't know Jesus. It may seem an impossible task, but with God nothing is impossible.

Flag of Senegal

PRAY:

- For a spiritual breakthrough in Senegal.

- For the 95% Muslim population to know Jesus.

DID YOU KNOW? 55% of people in Senegal are under 20!

FACT FILE:
Population: 13 million
Main Religion: Islam

Capital: Dakar
Official Language: French

ON THE MAP

DAY 38: MORE WORKERS

There are still so many people who have never heard about Jesus and are in need of someone to tell them.

The number of people groups in the world who have little or no way to hear the gospel is 6,645. This means that 6, 645 groups of people with their own language and culture have never heard about Jesus! This is about half the number of people groups in the world.

'He saw the crowds of people and felt sorry for them because they were worried and helpless. They were like sheep without a shepherd. Jesus said to his followers, "There are many people to harvest, but there are only a few workers to help harvest them. God owns the harvest. Pray to him that he will send more workers to help gather his harvest."'
Matthew 9:36-38

THE LISU TRIBE

Many years ago there were no Christians among the Lisu tribe in China. Missionaries such as James O. Fraser went to tell them about Jesus. People prayed for many years and now about half the Lisu tribe in China are Christians.

MANY NEED TO HEAR

More workers are needed to go and tell people about Jesus. We can pray with confidence for workers because we are asking for the very thing that Jesus told his disciples to ask for. Workers are needed for many different jobs such as evangelists, teachers, builders and medical staff.

PRAY:

- For more workers to tell people about Jesus.

- For people groups who have never heard the gospel.

DID YOU KNOW? The country with the most unreached people groups is India!

GET INTO IT

Rearrange the letters to find out some of the jobs that missionaries do. The first letter is in black. [Answers in back of book]

1. TLOPI

2. ECHETAR

3. TSTDIEN

4. RENSU

5. COTROD

DAY 39: UNITED KINGDOM

The United Kingdom [UK] is a union of four countries, England, Scotland, Wales and Northern Ireland. It consists of two main islands, Britain and the northeast of Ireland.

'Won't you give us life again? Your people would rejoice in you. Lord, show us your love. Save us.'
Psalm 85:6 – 7

In the past it has contributed to the spread of Christianity by sending out many missionaries. Recently it has blessed other countries in the world through the Alpha course (a course for people wanting to find out about Jesus) the 24/7 prayer movement and through many Christian writers and worship leaders. However, there has been a fall in Christian values. Few people now believe in God or go to church.

Flag of United Kingdom

Life in the UK has deteriorated and has left people feeling discouraged about the future. The UK has one of the worst levels in Europe for drugs and violent crime, and there has also been a breakdown in family life. Many Christians are praying for revival and for God to change people's lives as he did for a young man called Darrell Tunningly. He was a criminal and drug addict who did an Alpha course while in prison. He met Jesus and his life completely changed.

NEW WORDS: ★ 24/7 prayer movement – a non-stop prayer meeting.

PRAY:

- For revival in the UK with many people turning to Jesus.

- For Christians to be passionate for God and to share the gospel with boldness.

DID YOU KNOW? The River Thames which flows through the capital city, London, has over 200 bridges and 24 tunnels!

FACT FILE:
Population: 62 million
Main Religion: Christianity

Capital: London
Official Language: English

ON THE MAP

DAY 40: THE WORLD

We all know that the world is huge. It covers about 150 million square kilometres. There are about 7 billion people in the world, made up of 16,350 people groups speaking 6,909 different languages!

'For God loved the world so much that he gave his only Son. God gave his Son so that whoever believes in him may not be lost, but have eternal life.'
John 3:16

Did you know that Christianity is the largest religion in the world? In recent years it has grown faster than any other world religion especially in Asia, Africa and Latin America.

Today, 32% of the world is Christian!

We are told, however, that there are still 2.84 billion people who have yet to hear the gospel. The Bible tells us to pray for the world and for those who do not know Jesus.

About 30 years ago, the countries of Mongolia and Albania had very few Christians. They were thought to be places where it was difficult to tell people about Jesus. Many people faithfully prayed for these countries for a long time. Today, there are at least 40,000 Mongolian Christians and Albania is now open and churches are growing.

7 BILLION PEOPLE....

PRAY:

- Thank God for the many who have become Christians recently.

- For the continent of Europe where the number of Christians is decreasing.

- For everyone to have an opportunity to hear the gospel.

DID YOU KNOW? Over half of the world's population live in cities!

PRAY FOR THE WORLD!

WORLD CHANGERS 32% of the world is Christian!

PRAYER REMINDERS

Tick each day once you've prayed for that country, people group, or issue.

Day 1 - Algeria

Day 2 - Translation

Day 3 - China

Day 4 - Fulani

Day 5- Russia

Day 6 - Poverty

Day 7 - North Korea

Day 8 - Muslims

Day 9- Haiti

Day 10 - Tibetans

Day 11 - Iran

Day 12 - Child Labour

Day 13 - India

Day 14 - Clean Water

Day 15 - Cambodia

Day 16 - Radio

Day 17 - Mexico

Day 18 - Prisoners

Day 19 - Turkey

Day 20 - Street Kids

Day 21 - Mongolia

Day 22 - Buddhists

Day 23 - Burkina Faso

Day 24 - Neighbours

Day 25 - Kazakhstan

Day 26 - War

Day 27 - The U.S.A.

Day 28 - The Internet

Day 29 - Japan

Day 30 - Malaria

Day 31 - Albania

Day 32 - Students

Day 33 - Yemen

Day 34 - Refugees

Day 35 - Thailand

Day 36 - 10/40 Window

Day 37 - Senegal

Day 38 - More Workers

Day 39 - United Kingdom

Day 40 - The World

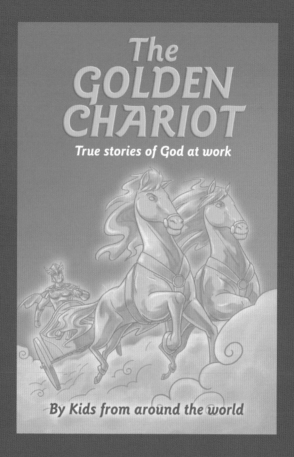

THE GOLDEN CHARIOT

These are exciting, true stories, written by modern day kids whose parents are part of a missionary organisation that is now 100 years old. These young writers reflect the multinational identity of WEC: they come from Australia, Peru, Brazil, South Africa, Germany, Korea, the Netherlands, New Zealand, Nigeria, the United Kingdom and the United States.

ISBN: 978-1-84550-981-1

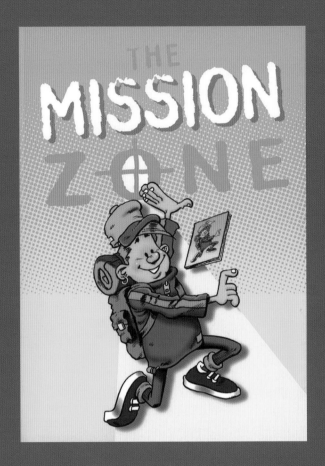

THE MISSION ZONE

Get your children interested in mission by using this excellent Sunday School resource book. Let your 7-11 year olds discover new cultures and meet colourful characters.

A creative blend of facts, games, crafts and ideas. User friendly and flexible. Easy to adapt to fit the needs of your group. Ideal for dipping into or using week by week. All you need for a five-minute slot or a two hour session.

'Cor! Cool!' Shona Clements, age 11

ISBN: 978-1-85792-446-6

COPYRIGHT OF IMAGES

Day 38: Quiz answers

1. Pilot

2. Teacher

3. Dentist

4. Nurse

5. Doctor

THANKS TO HAITIAN
STREET KIDS, INC. FOR
THEIR STORY ABOUT
STREET KIDS ON PAGE 46.

Christian Focus Publications publishes books for adults and children under its four main imprints: Christian Focus, CF4K, Mentor and Christian Heritage. Our books reflect our conviction that God's Word is reliable and Jesus is the way to know him, and live for ever with him.

Our children's publication list includes a Sunday School curriculum that covers pre-school to early teens, and puzzle and activity books. We also publish personal and family devotional titles, biographies and inspirational stories that children will love.

If you are looking for quality Bible teaching for children then we have an excellent range of Bible stories and age-specific theological books. From pre-school board books to teenage apologetics, we have it covered!

Find us at our web page: www.christianfocus.com

WORLD CHANGERS

World Changers is a network of Christian mission organisations including WEC, OMF, OM, Serving in Mission and ReachAcross. They work together in the south east and other parts of the UK organising events to encourage people to get involved in world mission.

Follow them	Online	worldchangers.me.uk
	Twitter	WorldChangersEvents@worldchgevts
	Facebook	facebook.com/worldchgevts